To: Michelle

I hope you enjoy reading
my spiritual journey and I
hope it helps you at
this difficult time of
your loss.

Love.
Judy

Healing Messages of Love
from the Spirit World

Healing Messages of Love from the Spirit World

Judy Magnussen

iUniverse, Inc.
Bloomington

Healing Messages of Love from the Spirit World

iUniverse books may be ordered through booksellers or by contacting:

iUniverse
1663 Liberty Drive
Bloomington, IN 47403
www.iuniverse.com
1-800-Authors (1-800-288-4677)

ISBN: 978-1-4620-6131-0 (sc)
ISBN: 978-1-4620-6130-3 (e)
ISBN: 978-1-4620-6129-7 (dj)

Library of Congress Control Number: 2011918831

Printed in the United States of America

iUniverse rev. date: 10/18/2011

To My Children:

You have been with me through all my tears and joy. I love all of you and am grateful to have had the opportunity to share in your lives from childhood. I feel very fortunate and honored to have been able to watch you grow into the exceptional men you are now.

To My Mother:

Thank you for all the love, support, and strength you have given me.

Acknowledgments

Special thanks to Danny Burns, the amazing artist who created the wonderful artwork for my cover page and the sketches in this book.

Thank you to my supportive friend Carol Erickson, who edited my words and encouraged and inspired me to complete my book.

Contents

Preface

I was born and raised on the west coast of Vancouver Island, where the main industry was logging and fishing. I have lived near the water most of my life and have always felt peaceful when I was close to nature. Life was simple when I was growing up. We made our own fun by skipping, playing hopscotch, building forts, playing marbles, or going to the beach.

My dad died when I was eight, leaving my mom with four young children to care for. In my youth, I had trouble dealing with the loss of my dad. I always felt like something was missing from my life. I married at nineteen and had three wonderful sons.

The beginning of my spiritual journey began at age twenty-two when I was awoken from my sleep and saw my deceased dad appear in the doorway with an aura around him.

Several years later, I divorced and moved to a larger community, where I was employed as a secretary.

While searching for the missing part of my heart, I made lots of wrong decisions. I attended a grieving workshop, where I discovered a lot about myself and learned to release the pain I held inside me. I was invited to a matrix healing workshop and started to become more spiritual.

I started to journal because I found it to be quite relaxing. One evening, my pen took over, and I was being channeled through automatic writing. (Automatic writing is when we allow information to come through our hands from our higher selves or from the other side. We are not consciously aware of the content.) Through this message, I was told to complete my genealogy. This message inspired me to search out and discover all I could about my ancestors.

My spiritual journey was sparked because of my excitement over the discovery of my Norwegian, West Coast Native, and English ancestry. My ancestors helped to make me who I am today. I am so grateful that I listened to my heart and continued on the search for my ancestors. I feel excited each time I learn more about them. I no longer have that empty feeling in my heart and now feel complete.

My new life of retirement will be filled with anticipation of new discoveries, and I'm certain it will be exciting. I feel blessed to have so many wonderful people in my life.

Enjoy your spiritual journey.

—*Judy Magnussen*

Introduction

I feel it is important for me to write this book and share my experiences and miracles with you. Many of you may have had similar experiences, but something held you back from talking about it. Perhaps one of these miracles will give comfort to you or a loved one, knowing our lives will continue in the spirit world once we pass on.

In my late fifties, I was becoming spiritual and wanted to help others deal with their pain. I took courses in matrix energy and balancing and discovered that my first-nations ancestors were healers

My purpose was to continue acquiring this knowledge. A friend offered to teach me some of his native methods that I could incorporate into my healing. People believed in me, and that gave me more reason to continue with my beliefs and what I was destined to do.

I started attending healing workshops and learned other techniques. I practiced on several people, and they said after my treatment, they had less stress and their pain had gone. I felt my healing energy was working, and I knew this was what I was meant to do.

I continued to work on my spirituality, and then I began to receive automatic writings. I feel blessed to have the ability to communicate with the other side.

A Glowing Experience

When I was eight years old, my dad died from leukemia. Several years went by, and when I was in my twenties, I woke up after a deep sleep and sat up in bed, crying.

I could vividly see my deceased dad standing in the doorway with a white aura around him. He just stood there looking at me as a proud, concerned parent for a few seconds, and then he disappeared. I couldn't believe what I had just seen, but I knew it was real.

I had never witnessed a spirit presence before. I felt blessed and excited because I knew my dad was not far away. He looked just as I remembered him when I was a small child. My dad had brown hair with a receding hairline, a manicured beard, and a wonderful smile that could be felt around a room as soon as he entered. He was handsome!

I was so proud of him and can remember the wonderful times we spent together before he became sick. I am so honored that he came back to earth to make a connection with me. I have comfort in knowing he is not far away and I will see him again one day.

My Message to My Dad

I missed my dad so much growing up. I wish I had been able to spend more time with him and do things like most kids get to do with their dads. When I look back on my life, I realize what an impact a death in the family can have on a child. I found it difficult to deal with the loss of my dad.

I always remember special things about him. One favorite memory I have of him was when he would come home from work. As soon as I saw him walking up our driveway, I would run to greet him for a big hug. Every night he would bring home in his lunch kit a chocolate bar with gold wrapping for me. When I go shopping, I glance over at the chocolate bar section and smile when I spot that special chocolate bar my dad brought home for me each night.

I longed to have contact with dad to see if he was okay. One afternoon I sat alone at the table and decided to write a note to the Creator and asked if he would contact my dad to see if he had a message to give me. I started journaling.

Dear Creator,

Please ask my dad to send me a message through automatic writing.

Dad soon responded with this message: "Yes, there is a message. I want you kids to know that I miss you all. I left you when you were all so young. I know you were at my gravesite and cleaned it up. You also discovered by doing your genealogy that my middle name was misspelled on my headstone. Thank you!

"I am sorry I had to leave your mom when you all were so young. Tell Mom that I love her and she has done a great job raising all of you. Please tell her to get checked after her fall and make sure she has an x-ray done. She will be fine. I know you kids love her lots and will spend time with her because she is so special. I want you to all get medical checkups and not let your health go undetected, as I did. I left it too long. I want all of you to stay healthy. I'm glad they have more cures now.

"I am around all of you to keep you safe and protect you from any danger. Please let the family know that I love them. I am near, but you can't see me. Life is fine here. It is peaceful and safe. Do you remember the stork postcard I sent you from the hospital? I know you will remember. Take care, and know I am not far away. Enjoy life because it is so short. In our time in the spirit world, it is just a flash, and I will see all of you again very soon."

After reading this message, I remembered when I was eight years old my dad was in the hospital. Before he passed away, he sent me a postcard with a stork standing on one leg. I will remember this forever. This actually reaffirms to me that my dad was speaking to me from the other side. I do not know what happened to the postcard, but I still have the memories.

The Rocks

S everal years after a friend's death, I decided I wanted
to go to visit his gravesite.

I had not gone earlier because it was still too painful
for me to acknowledge he was there. My friend Carol offered
to travel with me there by taxi. When we arrived, I realized I
had forgotten how large the cemetery was, and I had no idea
which direction to go. I asked the taxi driver to drop us off
at the office. I paid the taxi driver and thanked him for the
ride. When we entered the office, we were given a map and
directions to where my friend's plot was.

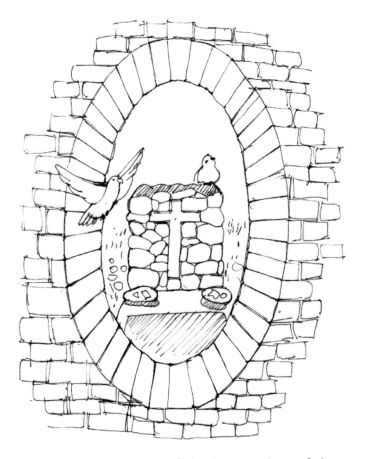

It happened to be one of the hottest days of the year, and we wished we had brought sunscreen and water with us because we were not prepared for the heat. We walked several blocks before we found the gravesite. We had to use our bare hands to remove the grass that covered the headstone. It looked like no one had been there for quite some time. I knelt down and talked to my friend as if he were there and apologized for not coming sooner.

Carol brought a book to read and leaned against a shady tree nearby. I placed two rocks that had messages printed on them on top of the headstone and asked my deceased friend to give me a sign if he knew we were there. Carol and I started walking toward the main road and caught a taxi back to our hotel.

That evening we decided to go out for dinner to celebrate finding the gravesite and having closure. We dressed up in our fancy clothes and went to a nearby restaurant. We arrived at seven o'clock and were escorted upstairs to the dining room to a table with a view.

In disbelief, I noticed a large rock on the table sitting right beside the salt and pepper shakers. I could not believe my eyes. The rock looked just like the one I left at the gravesite earlier in the day. Carol and I both commented to each other that it must be the sign I had asked for. We were both excited about what we had just witnessed.

We had a delicious meal of steak and prawns accompanied by a glass of white wine. For dessert we had a dish of trifle and Irish coffee. After dinner, the waiter arrived with our bill.

He said, "I do not know why there is a rock on top of this bill I'm bringing you." Then he noticed our facial expressions.

The rock had the same message on it that I had left at the gravesite. Carol and I looked at each other in shock because we could not believe what we had just seen. The waiter was curious about our reactions and asked us for an explanation.

We proceeded to tell him the story, and he said it gave him goose bumps.

I looked around as we left the restaurant and noticed that we were the only ones who had a rock on our table and bill. I felt so relieved that Carol heard my conversation at the gravesite and also witnessed the miracle at the restaurant. Carol definitely believes in the hereafter after experiencing these events.

Later that evening I wrote a message to my friend, asking if he was happy with our visit that day.

My pen started writing as fast as it could move. He was sending me a message. "Thank you for coming to see me at the gravesite. I want you to come and see me again and talk to me like you did today. My rocks are still there. I will leave some for you all around like you did for me. Life is so short, and you must enjoy the world and life. People have so much to learn from you.

"Your nana says hello, as well as your many friends who have left earth. They are all hovering over you. Please remember when you are sad that we are there to comfort you. We are all waiting for everyone to be together in the spirit world. You can't see us, but we are not far away.

"Your friend Carol is your guardian angel. Have you ever noticed that she is always there whenever you are in a crisis and knows when to help you out? She is amazing, and you are so blessed to have her. Treasure her, as most people do not have a great friend like that. Please look after each other. Her brother and mom say hi to her. They are with her lots and like to leave messages around for her. The bear is a comfort for her. Mom loves her family. Brian is fine, safe, and comfortable. They are together and want her to stop worrying and enjoy life."

All-Souls Spiritual Celebration

A few of my female friends and I traveled from different areas to have a girls' weekend retreat. We all met at a hotel early, checked in our luggage, and then relaxed for a few minutes.

We had several hours of free time before we had to be back for our dinner reservations at a favorite restaurant. Carol did not want to walk very far, as she was not feeling well and felt she might collapse if she was on her feet too long. She and her niece decided to find a bookstore in the area.

I mentioned to Marilyn, Carol's sister, that it had been two years since Carol and I had gone to the cemetery to visit my departed friend. I was curious to see if the rocks were still there that I had placed on his gravesite on my last visit.

Carol wished she felt better because she wanted to come. She still remembered the wonderful miracle we both experienced a few years before. Marilyn was excited to spend the afternoon outdoors with me and hoped it would be adventuresome.

It was on a chilly afternoon on October 30 when we arrived by taxi at the cemetery, and we noticed a man putting up lights outside the main office. I walked over to him and asked if he could help us find my friend's gravesite.

He said that it was unfortunate that the office was closed due to a special spiritual event happening that evening at 6:00 p.m. He said we were welcome to attend. He also said that there would be lots of workers in attendance and one of them would be able to help us out. He said that several computers would be on site to print maps out for family members and guests.

I told him that we did not have enough time to stay until 6:00 p.m. because we had dinner reservations with friends in another part of the city. I mentioned that we had to meet our friends at 3:00 p.m. and that I would really be disappointed if I couldn't locate the plot since we had traveled a long way by taxi to get there.

He said, "Walk over to the tall building across the street, and ask for Christy. Tell her that Roberto sent you over to see if she could help you out. She is tall, has long blonde hair, and is wearing short white boots."

As we arrived, we noticed several tables set up in the driveway with fresh flowers, ribbons, scissors, string, and tape on each table. Several people were preparing individual creations of long strings of flowers with ribbons on them to be hung around the graveyard for the celebration that evening. As we approached the group of workers, I asked, "Is Christy here?"

"Yes, she has just gone upstairs. Go right up!"

As we walked upstairs, one of the employees said, "You just missed her. Christy went out the side door and left to go pick up lunch for all the workers. Help yourself to coffee and sit down over there on the chesterfield and relax until she returns."

"Thanks," I said, "but we will go downstairs and see if we can help the workers in any way for tonight's festivities." Once we arrived on the bottom floor, we asked one of the ladies in charge if we could help until Christy arrived.

"Yes, of course. Come with me. The more the merrier! Let's find a table for both of you to work on, and I'll show you what to do. This is what your arrangement should look like. Here are all the supplies that you will need. There is an assortment of flowers over there. Help yourself, and have fun."

Marilyn was excited because she had never had such a spiritual experience like this before. A masculine-looking man dressed in blue took pictures of us as we worked. Several newspaper photographers were interviewing the organizers of this huge event. Both Marilyn and I were both honored to be participating in this special event.

Lunch arrived, and we were invited to join the workers upstairs for refreshments. We declined because we wanted to finish making our creations before we had to go. We were asked, "Would you like to be on the mailing list and come back next year to help out at this spiritual celebration for those who have departed?"

Marilyn and I replied eagerly in unison, "Yes!" We both had such a great experience, and the creations and grounds looked so beautiful. The surroundings were magical, with candles lit and flowers hung on trees that were blowing in the wind, and everyone was in such a wonderful mood. Marilyn and I really wanted to stay and enjoy the evening's festivities. I really enjoyed working on my project. I cut up strips of colored material to make bows and attached them between layers of roses and carnations. I secured the flowers by sewing them onto a long string.

Just when we were finishing up our projects, Mark, the cemetery maintenance foreman, pulled up in his golf cart. I greeted him and asked if he would be able to help us. He said yes.

I said, "We don't have much time, and we really need to find a plot number and directions where we can locate my friend's plot." Mark kindly offered to help find the plot number for us on the computer and said he understood our predicament.

After just a few minutes, Mark ran toward me with a big grin on his face, saying, "I found it!"

All of a sudden a man yelled, "Mark, come on, we have to go. We have lots of work to do on the property to get ready for tonight."

I was shocked when Mark ran past me to go to his coworker's vehicle. I ran fast and caught up to him as he was getting into the vehicle. "Did you find any information for me?"

He replied, "Yes, I did." Mark then jumped out of the vehicle and said to the man he was with, "I promised to help this lady out. I'll catch up to you later."

When Mark handed me the information he had found, I thanked him for all his help. I said, "Marilyn and I will walk over to the site now, and thanks again for everything."

Mark insisted on driving us. He said, "It is too far for you to walk. Get in my truck, and I will drive you." He then put a shovel in the back of his truck, along with a large rag in a bucket.

When we arrived at the location, Mark jumped out of the truck and ran ahead of us with his shovel and started trimming all the grass away from the headstone. He then took the rag out of the bucket and polished the headstone in case we wanted to take a picture for a keepsake. Marilyn took a picture with her camera, as I had left mine at home. Mark insisted on waiting for us in his truck while we were paying our respects. Right away I noticed that the two rocks I placed on the headstone a few years earlier were no longer there. I felt disappointed. I quickly slid a colored stone by the side of the headstone and put soil on it.

Mark, Marilyn, and I had such a lively conversation as he drove us back to the entrance gate of the cemetery. When we arrived at the entrance, Mark made arrangements for a taxi to meet us. That day was such an incredible experience for both of us. We felt privileged to spend such a memorable day with complete strangers who went out of their way to make us feel so special.

Marilyn and I laughed when we were in the taxi. We didn't think anyone would believe our magical experience and adventure at the cemetery. We were extremely grateful for Mark taking a few minutes to help us out. We thought he was such an amazing man. Marilyn and I were thrilled that we didn't leave there disappointed.

That evening we met our friends, and we all took a taxi to a quaint restaurant in the downtown area. We were escorted to a table. Standing right in front of our table was a musician playing classical music on his guitar. A masked couple dressed in Halloween costumes sat opposite us. Facing me on the chair in front of this couple was a man wearing a short black, blue, and white jacket outlined in sequins with the word "ROCKLESS" on the back of it. This caught my eye.

"Marilyn, do you think 'ROCKLESS' is a message for me because there were no rocks on the gravesite when we arrived?" I asked.

"Gee, I don't know, Judy!"

That evening I wrote in my journal to my friend in the spirit world asking if he knew we were at his gravesite that afternoon.

> Were you there when I was making flowers with Marilyn and the other workers?

My friend replied again: "Yes, I was. I knew you were there and saw you make a beautiful arrangement of red roses. I made sure you had a ride to the gravesite. I know you put a yellow stone by my headstone in the dirt. I am sorry the other stones got taken away before by the workers. I know you were disappointed. I was too. I was so happy to see you, and I felt tears of joy. I know you will be back again next year.

"It was so much fun watching you create a flower arrangement, and I was happy you didn't give up until you were shown where my headstone was. It was me in the restaurant when you noticed my jacket that had 'ROCKLESS' written on it. Yes, I had to give you a message somehow. I hoped you would pick up on it. You did. I was always with you but in disguise. Don't worry, we are all with you, and you will never be alone."

The Energy Healing Workshop

The night before I was scheduled to attend an energy healing workshop, I stayed with a friend who was also a healer. She proceeded to do a healing for me using a rattler and other healing modalities. After several minutes, she left the room. When she returned, she presented me with two eagle feathers.

She said, "Your dad came to me in spirit and told me I was not finished and that I had to present you with two eagle feathers." Afterward the healer was curious as to why I was to receive these gifts. She had no idea of my background. I proceeded to tell her that I had recently started on my genealogy and discovered I have some West Coast Native ancestry. She then understood why she was told to give me the feathers and said, "This all makes sense now." The message in this for me was to continue with my first nations' research.

The next day at the workshop, I felt like I had done this energy healing before and felt connected right away to the person I was working with. After I worked with several people, all of the people I practiced on told me that they felt relaxed and had no more pain. They told me that I had a special gift and they wanted me to work on them again. They also felt I had done this before and were surprised to hear it was my very first time.

The night before the workshop, I had a dream about my dad. He said, "You must not forget me." I told the others at the workshop about my dream because I felt it was significant to my receiving the eagle feathers.

Then, as music started playing, I could feel the presence of my ancestors with me, and I got up and started dancing a first nations' dance. I had never danced like this before. It was all new to me, but it seemed like I had done it many times before.

At the workshop, we learned how to do distance healing. When I was sending my healing message to my friend, I started chanting. I could feel a spirit presence. This was all new for me, but it seemed so natural.

Later in the afternoon at the workshop when we listened to music and meditated, I had an out-of-body experience— something I had never had before. I felt myself traveling at the speed of light around the world. I saw villages, towns, and resorts on the water and then went up into the universe to the Creator. I could feel this strong, bright light guiding me on the way. Others greeted me as I entered the bright lights, and our hearts joined. I felt relaxed as I floated into space. Afterward the universe was filled with an enormous heart. I could see my ancestors gathering in a circle below celebrating. I was not scared and felt at peace. I was in a meditative state until I could hear the workshop instructor call me down and ask me to go back inside my body. I knew then what I had experienced. I realized it was something special that so many people have not experienced before.

That weekend had an impact on my life, and I returned home feeling like a different person. I decided I wanted to heal others, so I soon had a collection of crystals, a set of pyramids, a rattler, a massage table, and other modalities to use for my healings. I then began to do energy healings on others. I had to learn not to take on their energy because I found it to be quite draining. I soon learned to anchor myself before doing any healings so I would not take on others' energy. I am grateful and happy I have been able to help others.

Automatic Writing

Another automatic writing I received was when I was trying to decide if I should continue with the search I was doing on my genealogy. I was sitting with pen and paper in hand just thinking, and all of a sudden my pen took over.

"You *must* complete your genealogy! Your dad wants you to do this and find out who you are and where you were derived from. He is proud of you and loves you. Your nana is here and is proud that you discovered her family and acknowledged their existence.

Nana

"Your ancestors want you to continue. They say that you will be fine. There is so much for you to learn. You must go to potlatches, learn about drumming, make shawls, and go to workshops.

"You will have lots of time when you retire. You will be able to give lessons and help others. You will travel to other countries, learn more of your heritage, and discover your roots.

"It will all be fine. You must do this, because no one else seems to be interested in doing your family tree. It will make everyone proud when you discover and learn about all the special chiefs and ceremonies. There is a lot for you to learn and so much more to discover. When you are here, you'll meet lots of those ancestors who want to show you more.

"All these things are happening by no coincidence. They are trying to make it easier for you to connect with others;

that is why they are all in your life, and you must learn from them. We all are connected. Enjoy your life, as it has no years, and we never know when our time is up."

My eyes filled with tears, and I was shaking as I realized what had just happened.

A Miracle

Upset and fighting back tears, I proceeded to tell my friend Carol that I just found out my son had been taken by ambulance to a hospital that was two and a half hours away from where he lived.

"He almost lost his life today. He is scheduled for throat surgery with a top specialist as soon as he arrives by ambulance. I am leaving right now. I'm so upset, and I can't think straight. I have to go now so I am there when he arrives at the hospital."

Carol exclaimed into the phone, "Judy, wait! I will come with you. I will keep you company and make sure you are okay because you sound so stressed, and it would not be wise to go by yourself."

I told her to hurry because I had to leave right away. It was very serious. I ran around the house grabbing a few items of clothing and a toothbrush, and then we jumped into my car. I was very upset that no one had called me earlier to let me know about it.

On our way out of town, I stopped at a gas station to fill up the car and withdrew money from the ATM for any expenses I might have while I was away. We were then on our way to Victoria.

So much chattering was going on in my mind. I was wondering how my son was doing and if I would arrive in time before he had his surgery. I kept saying, "This is serious, very serious."

"Do you know what happened, Judy?" asked Carol.

I replied, "All I know is that my son drove himself to emergency room at the hospital because he had trouble breathing. His doctor at the emergency room is sending him to Victoria by ambulance right away. I don't know any of the details, but I'm his mother, and I need to be with him and make sure he is okay. I wish I had been able to travel with him in the ambulance to comfort him. We have to get there soon because I don't want him to be alone when he arrives at the unfamiliar hospital. I pray he will be fine. I can't lose him or any of my children. I love them so much."

"He will be fine, Judy, I know he will," reassured Carol.

I replied, "I plan on staying at the hospital as long as he is there. Are you sure you want to come?"

"No problem, Judy," Carol said. "My husband said he will come and pick me up tomorrow, so don't you worry! You have enough on your mind."

I had to drive the speed limit because the visibility was so bad and I always have a hard time driving at night. I was relieved to see that we were almost in Victoria.

"Carol, do you remember where the hospital is?" I asked. "I'm confused and don't know which direction to go."

At that moment, an ambulance with the siren on rushed past us. I decided to follow it, hoping it would lead us there. Fortunately, the ambulance went to the emergency room at the correct hospital, and we were so relieved. I immediately parked the car, and we ran quickly into the hospital. We sat nervously in the empty waiting room waiting for a nurse to let us in to see my son. I was crying when a woman with long, braided hair on one side came up to me and asked, "What's wrong?"

I said, "My son almost died today." Tears were rolling down my face.

She hugged me and said, "He will be fine. Just believe in the higher being."

I asked her if she was a healer, and she replied, "Yes, just call me Anna. I am a custodian at the hospital."

Anna—the messenger

A few seconds later, a nurse entered the room and led us to where my son was. She said, "Your son is in a lot of danger and must be operated on right away."

I was so grateful we made it in time to see my son before they took him away for surgery. As I entered the room, I was frightened. He had tubes down his throat, and wires were all over. He was hooked up to a heart monitor and other machines that were observing him. His throat was so puffed out and swollen that it looked like he had no neck. Tears were running down the sides of his face. I felt helpless because my son was crying, and I tried hard to hold back my tears.

He could not talk, so he motioned for me to give him a pen and whiteboard that were sitting on the table. He wrote, "Mom, I almost died today."

I felt a big lump in my throat. Holding back my tears, I told him, "You'll be fine. I love you, and the doctors will be operating on you soon. Don't worry. I will be here when you come out of surgery."

A doctor entered the room and explained to my son what would happen in his surgery and that he would be in good hands. Carol and I were told we could stay in the room all night with my son until he was out of danger. I kept pacing back and forth, looking at the clock on the wall, wondering what was happening. I wondered, *Why is my son not back from surgery? He has to be fine.* I prayed, "Please, God, please don't take him away. I can't lose him. He is so special! He is too young to go. It's not his time. Take me if someone has to go!"

Carol noticed how stressed I was and offered to go get me some coffee.

I kept checking the clock. Two o'clock, three o'clock … I started crying and couldn't stop. *When is he coming back? I just need to know what's happening,* I thought.

Carol reassured me that my son would be fine. She said, "He has the best doctors and nurses working on him; just believe."

A few minutes later, my son was brought back into the intensive care unit, where we were anxiously waiting. He was medicated and going in and out of consciousness. There were tubes coming out of two parts of his neck. He had a drainage tube put in his neck as well as an incision with a tube in his trachea so he could breathe. The doctor said my son was lucky to be alive. He had a high fever, and his heart rate went up and down during the night.

I tried not to panic and kept wiping his forehead with a cool cloth to keep his temperature down. I kept squeezing his hand to let him know I was by his side. I felt that this was the worst nightmare a parent could ever experience. I was grateful my dear friend Carol was with me to comfort me. This was the longest night I had ever experienced.

When my son was asleep, I left the room to phone my other two sons. They said they would catch the first ferry in the morning. I started to cry.

At 8:00 a.m., Carol and I were asked to wait in the hallway while the doctor examined my son. We walked down the corridor a little way when Anna appeared to the right of me. She asked, "How is your son doing?"

I said, "He's not doing very well."

Anna said, "Believe in the higher being and he will be fine."

I noticed that both times we met Anna, she did not ever have a cleaning cart with her. A few minutes later, we were called into my son's room. The doctor told me that the situation was very serious and that my son would probably have to stay in the hospital for five to six weeks.

A nurse entered the room and asked us to leave so she could do blood work. She asked us to wait in the hallway.

While we were standing in the hallway, Anna appeared again. She said, "I am not only a healer, but I'm also the messenger."

Five minutes later, a miracle happened. I was told that my son was going to be moved to a room on the second floor. I was confused because moments earlier we were told that my son would have to stay in the intensive care unit for quite some time. We waited near the elevator so we could go with my son when he changed rooms. When the door opened, I saw my son sitting in a wheelchair. When I had seen him just minutes earlier, he was lying in a hospital bed in critical condition.

Carol and I followed closely behind as my son was wheeled to a room on the next floor. We were now in the old part of the hospital. He was definitely not in the intensive care area anymore.

On the wall opposite the room where my son was placed was a hand-drawn picture of Anna with wings. She appeared to be his guardian angel, and he could see the picture of her from his bed when his door was ajar. The picture on the wall looked just like Anna, the cleaning lady who appeared all the time, except that in the picture, she had wings. Was she really my son's guardian angel?

The next morning Carol's husband came to pick her up at the intensive care unit and was greeted by Anna. They had never met before, yet Anna took Carol's husband to where we were on the second floor. Five minutes later, a friend arrived, with Anna leading him to my son's room. Then my other two sons arrived at the hospital. The room was crowded. I was exhausted from no sleep the night before, so I decided to go to the family room down the hall to rest on the chesterfield. After my fifteen-minute nap, I returned back to the crowded room.

My son could not talk due to the trachea and drainage tubes inside his throat. He had a hard time coughing and looked like he was in a lot of pain due to his raw throat.

Again he motioned me to give him a pen so he could communicate. He scribbled some things down. He was worried his vocal cords might be destroyed. His throat and cuts would have to heal first before he could find out. That could take time.

I asked my son what had happened to him before he ended up in the hospital.

He wrote, "I was not feeling well a few days before. I had a swollen throat, so I went to see my doctor. He told me to go home and rest and ride it out because it was a virus."

My son does not get sick very often. He was in bed over the weekend trying to sleep it off so he would recover fast.

He continued to write, "I woke up at seven o'clock in the morning gasping for breath because my neck was all swollen and I couldn't breathe. I was at home by myself and wanted to call 911, but I could not talk and did not realize help would still come if they could not hear me. I jumped out of bed and ran for the mirror in my bathroom. I tried pushing for an airway. I was frightened because it was hard trying to find an air pocket.

"I can remember that it seemed I was watching myself from a distance above the floor and I saw my family picking me up off of the floor. I knew I had to do something. Fighting for my life, after pushing hard on my swollen throat, I immediately found a small airway and drove myself to the hospital, which was ten minutes away.

"I arrived at the hospital, and the emergency staff sedated me and I don't remember anything after that. I was told they put a tiny tube down my throat for an air passage. I was immediately transported by ambulance to Victoria."

The next few days were very stressful waiting until my son was no longer in danger. I was so thankful my family and dear friend Carol were there with me during the stressful days. I realized family, friends, and health are more important than all the money in the world.

Six days later, I was still by my son's side when his doctor walked into the room and said, "I'm really pleased with your recovery. Your tests are good, so you can go home today."

What a miracle to be leaving the hospital so much sooner than we were told a week ago. It was Easter morning—another miracle. I felt blessed by the higher being and was grateful for my son being given another chance at life.

This event has been a life-changing experience for all of us. It has had a major impact on my son's outlook on life. He does not sweat the little things and is happy to be alive. He is such a gifted man with many talents. I feel it was not his time because he has an incredible gift of music and must share his gift with the world.

I believe there was some help in my son being saved. I am extremely grateful for the incredible doctors and staff, because if it were not for them, he would not be here today. I also feel Anna, the messenger, had a big part in all this.

Miracles do happen … and it's up to you if you believe it or not. Carol and I believe that it was no coincidence that Anna was at the hospital to greet me, and we both feel she had some part in the miracle of saving my son's life.

Thank you! May everyone be blessed with love and appreciate those around you. Tell them you love them often, because you might never have the opportunity again when unexpected events happen.

Do you believe in miracles? I do!

Step-Dad's Departure

Today was a sad day because my step-dad passed away. I will miss him dearly, but I am glad he left peacefully into the next stage of his life.

I began to journal again because I needed to know that he was okay. I sat down with a piece of paper in front of me and began to ask my questions.

Dear Creator,

All of a sudden my hand started to transcribe his message. My step-dad said, "I am grateful for the healings you gave me. They helped to prolong my life. I was not ready to go earlier, and I had to have extra time to say my farewells. I am honored to have had you in my life.

"I am at peace, and I have messages to give to the family. I am okay, but I was too tired to hang on any longer. I am fine, and do not worry. A lifetime goes by so fast, and I will see all of you again soon. Your mom will be fine because she has all of you kids to look after her.

"I was greeted by friends who were with me before I departed, and they led me to the other side. I will be fine and will see all of you one day.

"I want to thank everyone for being by my side before I passed. This brought great comfort to me. Tell your mom I know she was sleeping by my side to comfort me before I passed. I want everyone to have a glass of wine for me. I love all of you!"

Waiting

D o you ever wonder why those who are close to death sometimes hang on? I've also noticed that sometimes they look around and take count of who is in the room before they leave. They ask "Where you are going? Where is ____?"

Sometimes they wait until the person they want to see arrives in their room and gives them permission to go. When the permission is given, a few minutes later the person dies peacefully. Their spirit then departs out of their body and travels into the universe.

It is amazing the strength of mankind and the determination to hang on to life for a person, a promise for an item, or whatever the reason that keeps people here. They feel their families must give them permission to die. They are suffering and want to say farewell to all of them, but not until everyone is ready to see them go. As soon as they see the bright light and the tunnel, their spirit is on its journey to the unknown.

As I watched a loved one on his death bed, I saw his spirit slowly leave his body. This was no longer the person I knew a few moments earlier. The color had changed on his face, and he was still. His body was just a shell, but his spirit had moved on to a greater place.

At that moment, I realized there was nothing to fear because he was at peace. It was hard to believe that he had gone forever. I know we will meet him again in the next dimension of life. Our Creator has a plan and helped him make his safe journey home. He is now reunited with all his friends and family who have already crossed over. What a celebration that must have been.

I have been told through my automatic writings that there are beautiful sounds of harps and cellos in the spirit world. There are no worries and only peace and tranquility. What a magical place.

Even though it is hard for those left behind, we must enjoy the adventures on the way. It can be heartbreaking to realize you can't pick up the phone and say hello or decide to drop in on your loved one for coffee. It is hard to accept that he or she is no longer with us.

We sometimes take people's lives for granted and think they will be with us forever. We should enjoy every day as if it were our last; that way we will never have any regrets by thinking, *I'll do that tomorrow.* That day might not come.

The Graveside

This is the day we all dread. It is the time when family and friends give their final respects and say farewell to those who recently departed.

I am not looking forward to saying good-bye to my step-dad. My mom will have to let her guard down because she has been so strong up until now. Mom will finally say good-bye to her loved one. Why do we all pretend that he has just gone away on a holiday or is visiting in the hospital?

I remember him sitting at his favorite spot at the kitchen table looking out the window. When I would leave my family's home, he would always poke his head out the window and wave good-bye. I enjoyed seeing his smile, and he brought happiness to my life. Those moments are no longer. He will not return because he has completed his life on earth. The truth is hard to face. His journey has taken him elsewhere.

Why does one have to leave to the next dimension? I guess our purpose is to continue to grow and learn as much as we can. The universe opens for us so we will be closer to our Creator. It will only get better.

The Bright Light

I had just returned home after visiting a friend when she phoned and said, "My husband said he has seen the bright light." Shortly afterward he passed away. He was worn out with exhaustion and pain, and when he saw the light, he just wanted to go.

I have heard of this happening to a lot of people. They say it is beautiful as they smile while reaching out to grasp the light to direct them to the other side. This reassures me that there is nothing to fear when leaving this dimension.

Surgery

I dropped in to visit my neighbor today. She said, "I have never told anyone before about the experience I had when I was a young woman and had surgery. I was partially awake during my surgery and could hear what was being said. I could hear the cutting of my flesh and feel the pain when they stitched me up. This horrible experience is something I will endure for the rest of my life. I remember seeing a tunnel in front of me that was trying to pull me into it. I had to pull myself back so I wouldn't cross to the other side."

I thought about what this person experienced and how traumatic it must have been for her. I'm sure others have had similar experiences of seeing bright lights and being drawn to a tunnel and having the choice of crossing over or not.

Our spirit does not die; it just goes on into the next dimension into the spirit world. We have to absorb as much knowledge as possible and take it with us for our next stage of our life in the unknown.

The Teacup

At lunchtime the next day, I decided to have a cup of loose tea in my fine china. Tea is one of my favorite drinks.

As I finished drinking my tea, I couldn't believe my eyes when I saw messages in small letters circling the inside of the cup. I immediately got out my magnifying glass to verify what I saw. This was my first experience with seeing messages in a teacup.

I was giggling to myself as I returned from my lunch break, and I felt so wonderful. I had a hard time keeping this secret to myself.

I contacted a psychic to see if this was what was really there, and the psychic told me it was and that I would be getting more messages. I realize that some people will not understand and will perhaps think I am crazy.

Another Teacup Message

I decided to go for a walk by the river with a friend. It was a beautiful day, and we both needed some exercise.

On our way back to the car, we stopped at a little tea shop because we were feeling thirsty and wanted to rest a few minutes. I asked for a pot of my favorite loose green tea. It was served in a special wide-rimmed gold tea cup and fancy saucer.

I slowly sipped my tea. I was surprised when I saw my name written in the tea leaves. I asked my friend what she read.

She said, "It looks like Judy with a heart above it."

I felt so honored to have this connection with the spirits. I realized this was just the beginning, and I feel I will be getting many more messages for me to communicate with the spirit world, as well as messages to pass on to others, loved ones, and friends.

Letter to my Friend

I have several friends who have passed into the spirit world, and I decided to ask them some questions. I started writing in my journal:

Dear friend:
- Why does everyone have to depart so young?
- Is it beautiful and relaxing on the other side?
- Are there any homes there?
- What is it like there? What do you do?
- If you are here by my side, please answer all these questions because there is so much I need to know.
- Is it similar to here? What is different?
- What do you do in the daytime and at nighttime?
- Are you all in body form or just spirit?

Letter from the Spirit World

And then a letter came.

"You want answers to all these questions! Well get some paper out because you will be writing a lot. It is beautiful here but not quite what I left. We all have our own space. I keep busy in the day making my surroundings beautiful. I like to keep busy most of the time and do not stop much. People drop in to see me all the time. I need to have them around. We are in spirit form and we can see each other.

"It is peaceful and serene. Most of the people are happy and always go greet those who are crossing and help them cross over. We are all here for a purpose. We are all equal here, and no one is bad. We all suffered on earth, and we are now in spirit form. We can go anywhere in a short time. We travel the world in a flash. We have no time here. We are all close by, and we try to let you know we are nearby without frightening you. I hope your days are wonderful. Don't forget to be present in your world because you have to experience all life has to offer. We are all here for a reason and have to find out what it is."

More Automatic Writings

Ihave been asked by several people to do automatic writings to see if I could connect with their loved ones. One lady asked if I could see if her husband had a message for their son because he was getting married, and she wanted to give the message to him the day of his wedding.

A message came through, and it said, "Tell my sons I will be there watching the ceremonies and I am so proud of them." My friend was so grateful.

At her son's wedding reception, his father's name was brought up several times. People said they knew he was there in spirit to share in the celebration.

On another occasion I wrote a letter:

> Dear Creator:
> Are there any messages from family or friends in the
> spirit world who want to relay a message to their loved
> one?

The following is part of the message I received from a person who committed suicide.

"Please tell my family I am sorry that I put them through so much pain by ending my life. At the last moment I changed my mind, but it was too late and my spirit had already left my body. I want my family to know I love them so much and am very proud of all of them. Please let them know I am always around to protect them. I am fine and will see them all again one day. Please tell them to love one another and enjoy each moment they have in this lifetime because it is very precious."

When I relayed this message to his family, I could sense their gratitude and closure because they knew their loved one is fine. They are at peace knowing they will see him again one day in the spirit world.

I feel if people just had one more moment to think things out, perhaps they would change their minds, like in this instance. We should all be sensitive to people we meet because no one knows what is going on in others' lives. If we only take a moment out of our day and smile or say hello, even to strangers, this could perhaps help save a life.

Life Is a Journey

I received this message from the spirits to share with others.

"Life is a journey, and we all need to connect with the spirit world. We all have beliefs, but in reality, we are all one in the Creator. We are all treated the same here, and there is lots and lots of space for everyone. Our lives are less stressed than on earth. There are no money issues because there is no money. Light is bright here. We still meet and gather for socializing, just like before. I know you will love it here."

More Questions!

I began to ask more questions as I sat journaling to the Creator for answers from loved ones who are in the spirit world.

- What was your experience when you arrived in your new world? Who greeted you?
- How have they been after so many years? What are your lessons?
- How long after people die are they up in the next dimension?
- Do you meditate often? Should I meditate more?
- How far from here do you live? How long does it take in time to get to me?
- How do you know when I need you?
- Do you connect with others?
- Do you have any messages for me?

The automatic writing began: "Yes, I have lots to tell you. You know it is a paradise here. Life is beautiful. Get out and enjoy the fresh air, water, and life. Do as much as you can outdoors, but always remember to keep in touch with friends. I am finding all my friends who are here, and we are reconnecting, which is great. We all have such great experiences and wish we were with our families. I know your purpose is to help others connect to ones on the other side. They are not far away.

"Walk near the water because it all connects to the universe and spirituality. Keep on with your meditation. Reading auras will be fun. You will see a lot. Your teacups are making sense, and you will see messages that have been sent. We will leave you a lot more messages. This is our way of connecting to you. Just accept these changes. It is all about learning, which is important. You will be doing a lot of healings, messages, and automatic writing for people because that is your calling. So many people from here want to send you messages to pass on. You are our interpreter, and I'm glad we have found a way to communicate."

Spiritual Retreat

C arol and I flew up to the interior to attend a weekend spiritual awareness retreat. When we arrived at the location, we signed up for the healing oasis, which consisted of sessions of energy work, intuitive readings, reiki, etc.

A psychic told me that I needed to open up my energy for more light to come in for my healings. She said I was an angel and my wings were crammed into a small box and stuck and they needed to come out. After an energy treatment, I felt so much better and more open to things.

In the morning, I was drawn to a sunrise ceremony where I was smudged before going inside the building. Smudging is where a combination of sage, sweet grass, tobacco, and cedar bark are placed in a shell and burned. A person waves a large feather to direct the smoke around a person to cleanse him or her, as well as to cleanse his or her jewelry and other items. It can also be used to clear a home of negative energy.

I joined a group of people inside, and we sat in a circle. Our leader passed around a large wing eagle feather. We each took turns holding it as it was passed around.

The feathers were soft and silky, and it was a very special moment for me. Earlier that morning my dad came through in one of my automatic writings. He wanted me to connect with my ancestors.

Our leader started singing and asked anyone who knew the songs to please join in. I started singing out loud and was amazed that I knew the words. I felt as if one of my ancestors' voices was coming through me. We were all asked to say a few words, and I talked about my purpose for being there and about my journey.

When our session was over, I hugged my leader, and she asked me to hold the wing of the eagle as long as I wanted to. When doing so, tears poured out of me, and the sides of my face were all wet. This was an important event to me, and I knew more was to come because my ancestors were connecting through me.

After I left this building, I headed over to another building where we all gathered for breakfast. As I was standing in line for my food, a lady in front of me turned around and brushed my arms, as if I had feathers on for wings. She smiled and said she was receiving such great energy from me. When she was leaving, she came back to me and stroked my arms as well, just like angel wings.

After breakfast, I attended a workshop that was called Complete Cellular Mind Body Alignment. This was so powerful. We each had a partner and were instructed how to do CCMBA. When my partner was working on me, I cried out loud, trembled, and coughed until I was exhausted. I had to release all my pain, torture, etc., that I experienced in my previous lifetimes as well as the pain felt by my ancestors.

Just as my last scream happened, I felt like I was a bird and my wings were breaking out of a box. I started flapping them with delight. This all makes sense now, as the night before I was told that I just had to let more light into my energy so I could break loose and be free. After this experience was over, I felt at peace and extremely tired. I had removed all the pain I held inside of me and could now get on with my life.

Everyone there was on his or her own individual journey. After this session was over, I walked back to our rented cabin to rest because this had taken a lot out of me. I had to rest and think about what had just taken place.

In the afternoon I decided to go to session called "The Art of Intuitive Writing." This was just what I needed to calm me after the intense session I had earlier. We sang, talked, and then meditated on a sentence that was written on the front of our books. My sentence was, "Eagles soaring on top of the mountaintops."

After a few minutes of closing my eyes and imagining the eagles flying over the mountaintops, my hand started to write quickly. We were asked to write one paragraph, but I couldn't stop writing until I had done four pages. I learned so much from this gifted writer who taught us many different techniques to writing and how to have fun with it. I am ever so grateful for this wonderful opportunity.

The next morning I woke up early because I wanted to attend the sunrise ceremony. It was called, "A Time to Give Thanks." Carol and I attended the ceremony. As we walked over to the building, people were lined up outside waiting for our facilitator to arrive. After ten minutes, a large portion of them were tired of waiting and left to attend another event. I had a gut feeling that our facilitator would arrive and felt I had to wait for her. I felt there was a reason she was late, and it was to help me through my trauma. A small group of us went inside the building and sat there waiting for her to arrive.

She arrived a few minutes later and apologized. She brought a white buffalo head with her and a large feather. We all sat in a circle and gave thanks. We all connected and talked within the group and shared some of our experiences. I was acknowledged for being the voice of the group, and people thanked me for sharing. Our facilitator started singing and asked everyone who knew the song to join in. To my surprise, I started to sing. I sang quietly, and then my voice was loud and powerful.

After this session, we all went to breakfast. I looked at my magazine to decide on what session I wanted to attend in the afternoon. I decided to attend the one called, "Return of the Ancestors and Wisdom Keepers." We all met and sat in a large circle. A large wing feather was passed around. Someone started to play a drum, and another person was running her finger around the top of a crystal bowl. This produced a sound frequency that sounded like beautiful music. As the drumming started and the crystal bowl was singing, a powerful native voice came out of me, and I started singing. When the drumming got louder, I got up out of my chair and started dancing a native dance. A few seconds later, another lady joined me.

My ancestors were with me this weekend. I felt they were excited to have me bring back their voices. This was so powerful. I felt strong and in control. Afterward I was hugged by people in attendance and thanked for speaking what they felt inside them. This was a great moment for everyone in the circle.

I was exhausted from this weekend and the growth I had gone through. I had forgiven those who hurt me, and I allowed the light to shine in. I realize that out of darkness comes light, and by forgiving those people who hurt me, as well as forgiving myself for any wrongs I may have done, I had opened my heart and let the light in. I was grateful for all the knowledge and wisdom I had learned at this amazing spiritual weekend.

Native Shawl

I decided to create a native shawl and wanted advice on what to put on it, so with pen in hand, I began to journal again.

Dear Creator, Dad, and ancestors:

Please guide me. Tomorrow I have a friend coming to my home to help me make a ceremonial shawl with long fringes on the bottom and sides.

What design would you like me to make on it?

What was your tribe, and what animal or bird represents you and me?

I have to decide what design I will put on it and what color beads and sequins.

Please guide me with any information that you would like me to have and share.

I am open, and I enjoy your presence. I love you.

XOXO

All of a sudden, my hand started to write. "You must be a representative of us. We want you to make a shawl with a bear and an eagle. They are courageous and strong. The eagle should have a yellow beak, and the wings will be wide open while flying over the water. We are all proud you want to make this shawl because it is a part of who we stand for.

"The bear should appear in the yellow moon. It is very important to have the eagle. We will guide you as you make it. We are all in tears as you carry on your journey. You will not regret this. Your singing will come again, and we will help you as you do the ceremonial dance and singing with the natives. They will realize that the white man was a native. We are all one. It has been torture for both sides. We have all experienced pain. You felt it. It was torture for you, but we were with you by your side. We cried for you a lot, but it had to be released so we could be set free.

"All your generations can now live in peace, joy, and love. This is a big, important step in your journey to connect with the new world. All mankind will eventually do this. Some are slower than others. You must go speak to the natives to let them know the journey you have been on and what has happened. It is a part of who you are. It is showing you really had a grandmother who was native. You are to be proud of who you are. Do not settle for less. Speak your voice. Do not accept blame if you have not wronged others. Help others to see the light. You are so open and will see a lot.

"Your healings are going to come very steadily now. You will be attending a workshop in the fall. It is important because you will go to villages and help those in pain to release their anger and illness. Lots of changes will happen. They will not drink as much and will have a new direction and be good parents because they can now love themselves and will love others wholly and unconditionally. You will love doing this, and it is a new journey.

"Many great things are about to happen. Your children have discovered so much about you that they never knew before. They are all excited for you and are proud. You asked what tribe you are from. It is called the West Coast Native Tribe. We lived in the Nanaimo area and Cowichan and are from the bird clan. You will learn so much more in the coming time. Your nana and dad are so proud, as well as their parents. They all have a voice now. When they existed on earth, they were humiliated, tortured, and treated awfully. No wonder you didn't know your nana was an Indian. Back then she would have been treated so badly, stared at, and made to sit in a separate room. They felt they had no dignity and felt unaccepted.

"Now you have taken charge of that, and you are proud of who you are and where you came from. You are not ashamed of your ancestors because they are part of who make up who you are, and what they went through has made you stronger and wiser. You are letting others know there is another spirit world and not to be afraid. There is more to life when one leaves earth. It will help all those who have to leave their bodies and go to the next dimension. I will be with you on this journey. This will help many people have closure over all their heartache. It is important to do this. They will be grateful to have this burden off their chest.

"You are an important, strong leader, just like the eagle. It is protection in full flight. Its feathers are soft, it is kind yet fun, and it will lead others on the path you took. We are all at peace. We love you forever. Don't forget us; we are all walking with you. Carry on, and it will be easier as each day goes by. Your sewing of this traditional shawl will be wonderful. You will then create a drum. Celebrations, potlatches, cedar hats, flowers, and smoke pipes are part of what you have yet to experience. It is so much easier writing through your pen. We are so blessed you are open to this. Learning to create moccasins will be another journey for you. Enjoy love and laughter because it is all around you. XOXO."

After several days, I finally completed my ceremonial shawl. I am so proud of it, and I designed it as my ancestors instructed me. I purchased enough black cotton material for the front of the shawl and the lining for the inside.

A friend helped me draw on the eagle and the moon and showed me how to put on the sequins and beads. I then slowly, one by one, placed sequins and beads on the outline of the eagle and the moon. After I did that, I decided to make a black bear in the moon as well. I drew waves of water under the eagle and sewed on a variety of blue beads and sequins so they would stand out. I stood back as I looked at my creation late at night, and I could see it sparkling in the light. This is the creation I wanted to make, and I am so proud of it and know my ancestors are as well.

Conclusion

My journey is all coming together with the discovery of some of my ancestors. I still have a lot more to discover. I plan on researching my Norwegian ancestors, traveling to Norway to see where they once lived, and learning more about them. This is just the beginning of my journey, and I can't wait to learn and discover more.

New messages from my automatic writing will lead me to unknown places. Stay tuned, and continue with me in my life of freedom and happiness as I write about my journey in future books. It is what we can all do together. Enjoy life. It is uncertain and a gift for all.

CPSIA information can be obtained at www.ICGtesting.com
Printed in the USA
LVOW100002131211

259075LV00001B/2/P